Tough Cotton

Tough Cotton

GORDONA BLOE

ISBN: 978-1-4834-3393-6 (sc)
ISBN: 978-1-4834-3395-0 (hc)
ISBN: 978-1-4834-3394-3 (e)

Library of Congress Control Number: 2015910166

Lulu Publishing Services rev. date: 7/15/2015

Contents

PART 2
WRINKLED SHEETS
THE LOVE INSPIRED INTELLECTUAL PROPERTY OF THE GORDONA BLOE COLLECTION.

This is for my prince, my sons, my precious metals, Zephaniah and SanDemetri. This is for my sisters and mainly Judith, who has been there for me through so much. This is for my nieces and nephews. I would like to thank my parents, especially my mother, and God for giving me life and the opportunity to experience it. I would like to thank my friend Aliaune T. for always telling me that I should publish my work from the first time I shared my material with him. Thank you, Dwan J., for your understanding and knowing how to use the right language to communicate honestly and effectively with me. Thank you for your unshaking stability and patience. Thanks to all of my nonbloed sisters and brothers for their positive feedback. RIP to my grandmother Mary; Novella (aka Cousin Boo); and my father, Phil. I love all of you.

Introduction

Have you ever been overwhelmed by life? Where were you supposed to go when it was all falling apart? Did people turn their backs on you when you thought that they would always be there? Do you have secrets that you are ashamed of or feel guilty about? Are you angry at someone? Did you do something about that anger, or did you keep it to yourself? Do you have regrets? Do you wish people would accept you for you? Have you ever lost someone you loved? Have you ever been in love? This book of poetry, lyrics, and stories contains raw experiences of those situations. It digs deep inside a wide variety of emotions and thoughts. I only ask that you stay open to love. There is another day to make your life better. Start at this very moment, even if it's little by little, to be happy no matter what you are going through or have gone through. This book will empathize, understand, and encourage you to keep growing as a seed through the dirt, storms, passion, and chaos until you become your own version of
Tough Cotton.

Special Note: The word "blue" and is intentionally spelled "bloe" through-out the book because of how part of my last name is pronounced and spelled. Therefore, it is linked this way. The spelling is native to the Netherlands and its former territories, such as the Dutch West Indies, where some of my ancestors migrated from when they came to the United States of America.

Also, "blood" is referred to as "bloed" within the book.

"Bloom" is spelled as "bloem."

Part 1

Chapter 1

Earth

It's Okay to Love

Everybody should have somebody to love. Love is the strongest bond. And if you don't have somebody to love, then I hope that doesn't last long. I love you so much. Open up and accept it before it's gone. The euphoria of love is so strong. Some people would do anything for the people they love.

Let's start with our mothers. Perfect or not, none of us would be here without them. Everybody has a different story. We may not understand everything about their ways, but because of them, we all have birthdays to celebrate. Our fathers may or may not have been around, but that's how the match worked out. It's okay to love your grandparents, if you're lucky to have them and they are still alive. They come with rich histories and unique stories that could change your life. You are blessed if you have taken the opportunity to find out before they leave. Talk to, hug, hold, and just love our people. It's okay to love our people.

We forget to stop and think about what we're doing to others. We're only concerned with ourselves. It's okay to love ourselves, but we have to give up love for someone else. It's okay to love our people today. It's okay to love our kids, parents, and others who take care of them. Know what this love is. When they go to school, it's okay to ask what they did. It's okay to be interested, whether you are around a lot or not. It's okay to let them know you love them. It's okay to love our brothers and sisters—brothers and sisters who are like our friends, and our friends who are like our brothers and sisters. It's okay to love our cousins—cousins who are like our siblings and friends. It's okay to love our friends and family. I'll say it again. It's okay to love—to love our people today.

It's okay to say sorry for hurting the ones you love. Just try hard to not do it again. It's okay to love our women and men. It's okay to show each other consideration. It's okay to do things for each other, like the things you know they enjoy. It's okay to ask what makes them smile. It's okay to make them smile. It's okay to love our people. It's okay to love our people today. It's okay. It's okay. It's okay to love people we don't know. It's okay to love our animals. It's okay to love this earth today.

To Be You

What is it to be you?
I am you.
In your eyes
I see.
I see someone I don't recognize.
The mirrors—the cameras, I believe—
they've all been telling me lies—
I'm fat, I'm skinny, ugly, and goofy—
then
showed me a pimple on my cheek side.
The mirror said it was nothing.
The camera made it look supersized.
Back to your eyes
reflect how gorgeous I am on the out,
which makes me feel pretty on the inside now.

Purpose

I am the descendant of my ancestors from around the world.
I come from them.
I am spiritual.
I am well connected to God, his angels, and his guides.
I plan to go to every place on earth that I can
and
accomplish what I'm supposed to in the flesh
before I return to the heavens.

My Prayer

Heavenly, grand Creator, I know it's been a long time since I've had a heart-to-heart talk with you. I know you've been watching me do the right and wrong things down here. On the outside I should be close to content, but my mind has been restless. I've been steadily progressing toward the goals society thinks I should reach. Who am I really trying to persuade? You, of course, know the truth, yet I've been ignorant and blind in my youth. In my mind, the thoughts were confused. You must've wanted me to do something strong in my life. I knew I could turn to you and ask for your help. You showed me ways to better myself. You never let me down. When I was seven, you sent those two girls to me. Otherwise, I would've drowned. You give me strength, endurance, power, and wisdom that are all around. This is the true love I have found. With this inside my soul, I hope that my art honors your crown.

Word

I'm in love with you,
Word.
Writers, poets, speakers, singers, lovers, lawyers, businessmen,
everyone, everything communicates with you.
I'm interested in knowing the next word to come out,
or have I had enough of the loud words, and do I
want to listen to my own internal words,
the silent ones
that I may say or prefer to keep to myself?
Our relationship is intimate.
I try to express my thoughts exactly by you. Word.
Sometimes I can't find the right word.
I am left frustrated, unable to attach the quiet word to
the word with the voice that I want to share.
There's only one of me and many of you.
You have a name called Word,
but we all use you in so many different ways.
Words break hearts, kill people, leave wills from the dead to the living,
send people to college or prison,
bond them through marriage and pure love,
or even separate them through divorce to try it all over again—
Perhaps never again.
New enemies, old friends.
Words can be sincere, critical, harsh, kind, in-
spiring, motivating, or entertaining.
Words give directions, make movies, list credits.
Word is the stamp in the ghetto to agree with a statement.
People have a tendency to look for the best word.
All words are perfect.
Not all words are perfect together.
People use words to get more words they want to hear or see.
Some of us can feel words.

Energy.
Word,
You bring me pain, sorrow, joy, happiness, appreciation,
and so much more that assures me that I am alive.
God must be Word.
A word is everything, and if we didn't have Word,
We would have nothing.
I love you,
Word.

Strong

Stay strong in these hard times. I've seen them worse than this before, never far from my mind, no matter how much I tried to keep it pure. This house is built of cement and hardwood floors. Persevere like I'm made for war, but I want to love. It's crazy that I have to fight to keep that love tough. The more we do, we can't get past the fact that it's never enough. I'm extremely exhausted from giving so much. Keep using the past like an old battered crutch. If this is love, I think I'll give it up. Straighten up my back and wish myself some luck. So how do you like me now? Hope that Phil is on my left shoulder—proud. Had it up to the neck, but I'll never forget. I keep these situations in check. Capture the strength from within. Grasp it with my fingertips. The touch tickles the skin. Awareness hits the brain, like it's always been. How are we living in a world of greatness and sinning? Never knew it could be like this before. Just wanted to get to know you some more. This life brings so much to the poor—pain and the bittersweet past we choose to ignore.

Ignoring it or ignorance can get anyone hurt, not using common sense. Trapped within the walls behind the fence, get a glimpse of the lifestyle we live. Which game do we want to play today? Flip—split these personalities like we're crazy. Who is the judge with the jury? Watch and listen for the rules they say—some easy, others complicated. Always remember what you've stated. Treat them as fisherman who keep their lines baited. Game— everyone says they hate it. Look at how many of them have been created. Wit—it's all about outsmarting them. Expose all characteristics—basic to ballistic. Who can remain calm and handle it? Now swallow the worm of pride while still escaping out of the net with your life. Slippery, dirty, yet satisfied.

Physical/mental/emotional strength—could I measure how much they could all take in length? At the gym I can only press but so much weight. I absorb the stress of each day. The conflicts of interest constantly go against the grain. Decisions—they never go away. I make them, and I'm still not sure if I'm going straight. I'm concerned. If anyone asks? I'll tell them I'm doing great. It's sort of a lie, but those doing worse will be my alibi. Sometimes at night I break down and cry. I start to feel stronger as my cheeks start to dry. I pull it together and continue to love this fight for life. I stay strong in these hard times. I've seen them worse than this before.

Ripped Label

Ripped the label off my forehead
that read
I was whatever they said.
I should be whatever they tagged
small, medium, large, brown, black, orange, or red.
In truth, I'm not that color or that size.
I get returned for not being the perfect fit.
You got it.
We thought we could handle it.
We were in a rush and had no question marks.
Today is the day we decide we don't want this at all.
This is where we started to slip.
We started to label the relationship
or rather me.
As a girl we do this too many times.
Where is this going?
Is this for real? Is this for life?
Am I your girlfriend?
You're sweet and nice.
Are you looking for a wife?
Am I yours? Are you mine?
Who am I?
These labels drive all the men I've known away.
As soon as there is one,
everyone starts getting strange.
Who does what which way?
Conditions on love—
How do you explain?
Like everything else God has made,
it just is.
I've been tried on.

Every day I have been worn
so much I look faded and torn.
I was never the description that was printed,
yet I'm now what they call vintage.

The Angels

He said he was leaving this world of sin
to start a different beginning.
Imagine all the places he's been—not quite like back then.
Didn't creep me out when he said he'd be back again.
Just how would I recognize him?
By the events that would happen.

I couldn't fully understand.
I had many questions whirling around in my head.
He told me, "Don't worry.
Now go to bed."

About to say something else.
He replied.
He'll be back when I really need his help.

So I nodded my head instead, planning on fixing those regrets.
Next was his last breath.

Unable to sleep that night from all the enlightenment,
yet, as the days went by, time eased up the excitement.

Usually it's the common scenes that make time fly.
Reflection takes place in the mirror.
Can't stop wondering what I am doing with my life.
Stare into those eyes,
and you look down at your shoes while you stand,
hands on the sides
of that young person.
No matter the age, it's just the same
mental pain—feeling insufficient from some kind of heartache.

What is in my path?
It's a question I had to ask.
This far along, I figured I'd accept it that way.
But one day I woke up, and all of that changed.
The water in the rivers flows so naturally.
That's how easily it comes instinctively.

Something inside the brain silently speaks.
Explain to the people what they need.
Actions show how to teach.

What do we think we're here for?
To show off how rich we can get in front of the poor?
That isn't cool anymore.

The angels point which way to go.
Without seeing, I sense what they want me to know.
I'm finally ready to grow,
just like the buds peeking through the snow.
It's the first day of spring,
the final days of the freezing cold.

The old life is dead.
I'm so excited with a new life ahead.

I can tell I'm moving in the right direction, by the positive progression.
I've learned valuable lessons.

The first is based on intentions.

Do everything for the right reasons.

Empathize when someone is grieving.

Respect breeds loyalty.

Ego and hate perish with humility.

Say it and mean it.

Live long. Hold on.

Give charity again and again.
You never know when you need a helping hand from a future friend.

These are the messages the angels send.

Chapter 2

Cotton Seeds

Precious Metals

My prince, my sons, I call my precious metals. Skin smooth as
chocolate pudding Jell-O. Say hello to my fellows. I'm trying
to make cast-iron pots with accents of gold and clear diamond
rocks. The family system is in chaos and shock. A matriarch is
on the throne. The father so far mentally gone. It's been too long
as a simple pawn. The tears I shed. The king, to me, is dead.
My prince, I said about the past. The present, my sons. The fu-
ture ahead. Beware of false friends. These people have debts.
An existence full of regrets. They can drain you till you've bled
to death. So let me give you this advice: a brief and concise con-
solidation of life from high above to deep below. My precious
metals should know their instincts, their strengths, the ener-
gies that flow. Be wise. Stay calm. Analyze these whys, these
lies, so many dimensions, the truths we find—the shape, the
size, beautiful and flawless—amongst the dirt, inside the earth.
Incredible worth for diamonds, platinum, gold, and silver- They
dig. They search. Bronze, coal, and oil- So dark, they say. We're
made from soil. Imagine the names they call us: blacks, mutts,
dirty, and spoiled. Like a slinky, I recoil. Carry yourself as you
are royal. Only be loyal to high standards and morals. Cash is
worth lust. Backed by faith, we shouldn't trust. Once upon a
time it was okay to steal and murder us; that's the part that was
twisted up. Evil is greedy. Our God is love, from birth to the
dust. My prince, my sons. I stay gentle. I call my precious metals.

I am your queen-, your Mother Earth. With your birth came
joy, came hurt. Your screams hit the air and verified your life—
brought tears to my eyes. Beautiful face—round as the sunrise.
Every new day, my sons rise—precious metals, part and even
black as a teakettle. Stay steady while everything around is unset-
tled. I've given you everything to make you so brilliant and strong,
rare and pure. These thieves will take what doesn't belong—the

land, the jewels, commodities. They raid. They claim it is theirs, for sure. From where they came, they were the shame and filthy poor. They only knew death and holy war. Civilized and barbaric, I stay silent and bear it. But you—my prince, my sons, my precious metals—I cherish. Every time you are born, I give you everything to inherit. The nature you see is yours to keep when you wake until you fall asleep. Material things can be stolen, but not the mental wealth you are holding. Always know, as you continue to grow, you can never reach too far. Be incredible as you are, and remember you're always covered by the stars. My prince, my sons. I stay gentle. I call my precious metals.

Did I tell you how much I truly love you? Well, here it is, and I'll say it over and over again. My prince, my sons, my men, my precious metals—you're absolutely everything to me. I gave you air so you could breathe. I gave you milk so you could drink and eat. I gave you water so you could stay clean. I made you such a beautiful human being. Though the tragedies you've felt. May this reassurance help. You are able to accomplish much by yourself, yet, even more, on the right team. Pay attention to keep your senses keen. Your brain can create such a wonderful theme; it can take you out of this world in your dreams. Bring it to light as you open your eyes. Sharing it with all is the ultimate prize. So I claim this. You are finally rich and famous. My prince, my sons. I stay gentle. I call my precious metals.

Upcoming Queen

Such a beautiful baby girl.
From slime and dirt
came a perfect pearl
on our date of birth.
Our parents might have thought they had failed,
believing pride is having several males.
So precious is our worth.
We've been put last; we should've come first.
Women are the strength.
They can go through pain for an incredible length.
Don't let anyone try to take it away.
We give them life; without us human life will dissipate.
Throughout the world
these babies are fighting to survive as a girl.
Never alone—set this in stone.
I didn't get it until I was quite grown.
I never had the kind of love I should've be shown.
Inside I developed so rough.
Over the years I lost a great deal of trust.
What has happened to us?
My skin is too light; dark is what I like.
My hair is almost black.
I've changed it to red.
I'm too thin. I'm well fed.
I got tired of the old color,
so blonde was what came next.
I did it for me, not to turn you on.
I'm too short. I'm too tall.
I learned a few lessons. I'm aggressive.
I had my back against the wall.
Nowhere to go,
I had no choice but to fight them off.

I'm at the mall.
Maybe I talk a lot. Dizzy I am not.
My phone rang, but I ignored your call.
I'm dependent. I don't need you at all.
I'm clingy. I'm aloof.
I'm getting old. I'm still in my youth.
There is something else that I am told.
I really don't get
how can I lie when I'm constantly telling the truth?
I have too many clothes. Why do I think I need another pair of shoes?
Is it the media, or is it me?
I'm not sure, so I turn off the TV.
I'm everything. Why doesn't he see?
Smooth and polished,
everything counts for this scene.
I'm redesigning myself to be the Upcoming Queen.

Queen

Born a beautiful baby girl,
the perfect pearl.
Precious is my worth.
I am a wonderful blend of my parents.
I love my family.
I am the strength this world has always needed.
I will persevere through the best and worst.
See me cry. See me smile. See the stars in my eyes.
I will be ready no matter what my height, weight, or color is.
I am intelligent, and I will win.
I daydream … I am thinking of the future.
I envision myself as being one of history's greatest.
I will have everything I always wanted, because I believed in myself.
I will do and be, because it all counts in this scene.
I Am Queen.

The King's Code

I love and protect my family.
I keep my word the best I can.
I do not fear what is out here.
My friends are also kings.
I respect my queens—that's every female on my team.
I study books and people.
I am strong and clean.
I walk, talk, and dress like a king.
This is The King's Code, and
I Am King.

To My Young

Some might not understand.
I couldn't put his bloed
on my hands to keep my plans.
I was too young for a wedding band.
I was so close to his age.
I could relate to his thoughts
while the size of a piece of grain.
Ain't no way—even at fifteen—
that I would have an abortion to induce his pain.
Cut up and washed down the drain,
I went through the motions and the weight gain,
breast-fed without being vain.
My decision changed everything.

People don't know why
some others have their young extremely young and ignorant
by bums or those on the run from the slums,
only to land dead or behind bars.
Find out that the end
is the only way to touch the stars.
Out of this universe in the same breath,
exhale curses, turn to blessings.
Positive attitudes produce the sharpest weapon.
The younger you are, the closer the relation
to the creator, the keener the senses
of what is right or wrong.
He's here for now, but not long,
so hold on.
Most perfect combination of our faces of mixed races,
the simplest earthly possessions
comfort humans in their favorite places.

Grilled fish, steamed apples with spices,
fresh water underneath trees near a stream
are the only other things we need to make our dream complete.
There are a lot of things we can live without,
but not the subtlest things
of the earth or the smallest form of mankind,
what I'm talking about.

On My Way with the Kids

It's Friday night. It just came out: one adult, one child, popcorn, extra butter, Muddy Bears, Cherry Coke … I'm on my way to the movies with my son. PG-13, rated G, 3D, Twizzlers, Skittles, pizza, bubble gum. We're at the cinema, watching action, comedy, and drama. My son's cute. He wants to see it all. The previews sparked it all. Right after the show, it's still early enough to hit the mall. Back in the car, he's going to text his friends what he just saw. It's the weekend. On Monday he's the first with it on. As we move along, he's matching his words to the song. We sit back as we ride and talk about life, like what we see. Some of it's funny to him and me. We both agree, even if we disagree, we're still going to be really tight. We're at the restaurant. My son can order whatever he wants. He loves shrimp cocktail, virgin strawberry daiquiris, steak, and croissants. I listen. I talk. I know my kid. I give it to him exactly how it is on our way home. After a long day, we're both in a zone. We're a little tired from all of it. I make him brush his teeth and wash his face. I put him in bed and tuck him in, let him know I love him and will see him in the morning.

I don't have any daughters, but I have some nieces. We're going to the ice cream shop to get a sundae on Saturday. Two different flavors, sprinkles, fudge, and Reese's Pieces. We're going out of town after this, but first we have to get a couple new outfits. Now we're on our way. My niece is going to make me play her favorite song list. It goes like this: We turn it up. We turn it down. She's got a lot to say. I listen. I say, "you talk a lot." She laughs. She says, "Auntie, you mean. You so crazay." From Atlanta, we drive to Savannah. Droopy leaves on trees and carriage tours. We're at the hotel by four. Towels and drinks set up on the stool. Hot tub. Pool water cool. My nieces are like their cousin; they order what they want. They order almost the same thing: shrimp cocktail, Arnold Palmers, steak, and croissants. We walk around the square, buy old-fashioned candy to share, and enjoy life without a care. Back in the room. Checkout is at noon. For now, there's nothing like a bath for a nightcap. Order an animated movie and set the remote control by our lap. I love my nieces. They know that. They make me smile when they laugh. They love me too. We'll do something fun again really soon.

This Generation

How do you expect me to raise our babies right without you here?
Your late nights out leave me with terror and fear.
Wherever you are puts scrambled thoughts in my mind that won't clear.

Did you forget that your actions create reactions?
I can see through what you thought you were masking.

Hopelessness, insecurities, and pain drowned in defeat,
like why the creep who left your man bleeding to death in a heap
is still moving in the streets.

Loved him more than your own brother,
you did.
How do you keep your respect, dignity, and morals when you have kids?
Who told you they'd be fine
if you had to do a bid?
The dead know not anything, so what can crime give?
A baby's mama is facing negligent charges,
but she insists that it was SIDS.
This ain't the kind of life to live.
Yet, it still exists.
Let's be realistic.
Most aren't even aware of the statistics.

I need you here running this house!
I know I'm strong and independent and can persevere—
that's not what this is about!
How can you move forward
if you don't put your foot down?
How dare you search this house like a bloodhound?
Where were you when you weren't around?
I thought you were lost, and look what I found—
your name with completed reservations in another town.

If I don't know, then it's not supposed to hurt,
yet if the electricity is off in the night,
sure enough in the morning the sunlight will work.
Dirt is dirt, and the only way to clean it off
is to make mud first.

You can barely feed yourself,
so why are you going raw
with someone you don't plan on making your spouse?
Why are you not concerned with your health?
How can you not question something when you have doubts?
Let me find out.

I love you. I love you, and I don't want you to die,
but you'll never know, because you're mastering your own suicide.
Do you think they don't know where the guns are that you hide?
Drugs blow out your mind and blind the third eye,
point-blank range between your two eyes.
You think you're large—
ha!
They have many more so many times your size.
What good is your alibi?
They already expect everyone in your crew
to back up your lies.
Even if it was the truth,
they prefer the wildest story that pays the highest price.
How about watching a generation of
mass suicide?

Learned Helplessness

Early on it was his mother and this gentleman,
not his father, so he would've preferred that he'd per-
ished before his life would begin.
There's no joy in a child who's not allowed to
make noise over the drop of a pin.

Living the life worse than hell,
only his unconsciousness would stop the yells.

Thinking to himself
he'd get even, getting smacked down so much,
that when he tried to walk the only thing he could do was crawl.
One day that gentleman pushed him too far back into the wall.
How he left that man was raw,
yet no one knows whether they should've gotten sick or start to applaud.

By now he was an extortionist.
He was pro-choice; he supported women's rights and abortionists.

His parents always said they wished he was born dead.
How their hopes vanished as his skin went
from purple and then turned red.

He believed them.
Reality plunged those statements deep within.
He never liberated himself, and nothing could stop him.
Prison started to control the way everyone around him lived.
They were monkeys in his eyes, the way people went out on a limb.
He liked his peers coked up and trim.
Loved everything that was grim.
Whatever it was, he was moving it in the pen.
He doesn't trust anybody, least of all his friends.

He's crying at night, because he's caged in and restless.
This is an example of learned helplessness.

Several babies' mamas by teenage daughters—
these girls are living so poor in their hood.
Most won't leave, even though they could.

Wrong daddy's name on certificates and don't give a damn,
she won't press the right man for child support in the biggest jam.

Besides the fact that I know details that make us relate,
I still recall my confused mental state.
This dude knows I'm too young and it's statutory rape.
He's on top, looking in my eyes, knowing he's changing my fate.
Nothing about this situation is great.
At the time he should be someone I can trust.
He's a grown-up, and he just said it was love.

Oh yeah, just like that, I'm in this trap.
By the time I'm sixteen I can work, study, and graduate.
Primitive society automatically moves chil-
dren into a man's or a woman's stage.
Look how I would behave.
My mind was childish. My body wouldn't open
up. The child's heartbeat was grave.
This is the baby who they would have to slice me and take,
buried under general anesthesia and barely taking a breath.
Bringing in life is the closest a woman gets to death.
All the women I know were brought up realizing this.
It's one of the first lessons we learn in helplessness.

God, please forgive. I'm just not ready for this.
But I just can't let this baby live.
Some people think I'm a stupid bitch.

What am I supposed to do?
My options are limited, and I have no clue.
I had to hurry up and choose.

One way or another, the decision is getting tougher.
My boyfriend left, so I can forget about a husband to take me in.
The teachers at school want to know where I have been.
I'm at church, asking God to forgive me for my sin.

What was good for them ain't in the plan for me.
They see joy; I see misery.

They see a bassinet, and I see me not getting any sleep.
They are playing for keeps; I hope I never see that creep.

I see a curse, and they see a blessing.
I may be selfish, but to me it is senseless.

To do this on my own while it's having tantrums on the floor,
people stare, and what is seen in their eyes we all try to ignore.
I can't see myself sweating, angered, and ashamed
of my own proved ignorance.
It's a past I'll soon try to forget.
This is nothing but a regret.
I hate that this is such a hot topic of interest.
It's a decision of turmoil to put your own flesh and bloed in soil.
I think back on how I got myself into this,
how I got myself backed up into a corner and learned this helplessness.

In Memory of the Lost Babies

Let's bow our heads in silence and pray
for the babies who didn't make it to this day,
God's children who were supposed to stay.
Please, tell me there's a better way.

She's fifteen and about to be a mama.
There's no way she can face the upcoming drama.
No matter her choice, she knows she's in for serious trauma.
Things are hectic at home.
The family can't even afford a phone.
Waiting too long will mean her cover is blown.
This can't get out to be known.

Besides, there's no place or love for another kid,
Or even anyone out there she knows who's willing to give.
Father of the child denying all of it—
be gone with it. I'm out of it,
damn it!
He couldn't care less
that she's about to go through more pain than be-
ing taken by an overgrown rapist.
It's tragic to be alone and not ready.
Ground shaky, legs wobbly, things on the table are hardly steady.
There's no way she can keep her balance.
Tears tear through her face until there's no longer any innocence.
She's so ashamed,
with everyone to hate and no one to blame.
Legs propped up, doctor paid,
the baby didn't make it today.

Mommy, why did you pay to kill me?
It was so warm inside.

I was so happy I could have made you smile.
If you stuck by me for a while,
I felt you tremble but couldn't hear you cry.

Then all of a sudden I felt a sharp pain.
Something sucked me up, and I went down a drain.

What could've been so bad?
I shouldn't be the baby you could've had.
I loved you from the day of conception,
'cause you were all I knew.
But, Mommy, why couldn't you love me too?

In this marriage for seven years,
we used to be a lovely family.
But these days, this man brings me nothing but misery.
I gave him two kids. Now I'm about to give him number three.
He's acting like he's stressed,
as if I put him in a mess.
All I put out was the best, and the grand Creator blessed.

However, evil always has a way of trying to switch things
by turning life into nightmares when we only
wish they stayed sweet dreams.
A man who once loved me, selling our wedding rings.
We argue every day, and he feels there's nothing to change.
Victims of society and we're all about to pay.

He should be treasuring me
forever into eternity;
however, lately it's assault and battery.
He killed my baby.
Tears, blood, and water were all over the place.
When I held my child and looked in his face,
this is what he had to say:

"Mommy, please, why didn't you leave?
You are all I need.
With all I had, we didn't need Dad.
He was nothing but trouble.
I could hear him and knew there was a struggle."

Then I heard you cry, "Don't let my baby die."
I tried to hold on inside,
but the pounding was too rough, the cord loosened, and I started to glide.
Even though I didn't make it tonight,
in my heart I pray you'll be all right.

I loved you from the day of conception, because you were all I really knew,
but, Mommy, why couldn't Daddy love me too?

Chapter 3

Bloeming

Bloeming is pronounced Blooming.

Before the Beginning

I want to introduce myself as history,
make things clear that seem blurry,
what I was before I got here.

The last name means bloed thorn,
so touch, get pricked by it, and watch the bloed pour.
Let me take you on a tour with this girl around the world.

Sometimes I think how it would be
to be with someone like him, someone like me.
I'm talking about *the big head of the Fed*,
and I could be similar Hetty Green, young witch on Wall Street.
Forget the block or even the city—
we are trying to control the whole economy.

Oh, but we're exotic, from all over this earth.
Ever since birth, it couldn't have been a curse.

At first, all of our ancestors lived the life of simplicity.
Then it was the ones living nomadic, making tepees.

Beautifully adorned in turquoise and fringed skirts of doeskin,
I am the daughter of the chief. I am the tribe's chieftain.
That's when I met him, next to the stream.
He was a stolen prince from Africa, sold into slavery.
He's on the run for his life but slowed down when he saw me.

Collar on his neck, scars on his face, and branded arms-
Strong as pharaohs guards,
I immediately felt safe.
My body language told him to follow me.
Watch us blend in with nature.

It's a long time before we see any type of civilization.
Deep, hidden in the forest, we started this nation.
Daughter born while husking corn,
in the times when dishes were made of animal horn.
Years later the tribe is slain.
It's plain. Rape is pain, so a daughter is soullessly made.
God, please let it rain.
Thunderstorm, your tears can express how my heart is torn.
Cut hair. Show them how we mourn.
Traded for goods, daughter now the house slave at a faraway plantation.

A couple sons for the master,
but they are watered-down creations, so they are not built for this disaster.
Let them go. Send them to the north,
two of the thirteen colonies, Jersey and New York.
Momma's now earthly departed.
She'll sleep better now that everything has ended since it started.

Gorgeous, young, intelligent men ready to start a fresh beginning,
female catchers when they're grinning.
Hard work, racist slurs from all sides, best and worst of those worlds,
easy sinning, wrong girl, bloody chinning,
love more than anything, then it's gambling,
application of thoughts, earn degrees in science,
numbers serve entrepreneurs' motivational guidance.

Sugarcane, sugarcane, I think sugarcane, cotton, and tobacco are to blame,
but wait!
The Dutch are in South America, knocking the natives out of the
brush, and they're getting the Africans over there in a rush,
yet that's not enough!
After they breed with the natives and slaves,
they act like they can't stand their touch.
What?
I am the product of such.
Figure this: when I'm around, they can't get enough.
Enduring cultural racism and the abuse has been rough.
Still, I have to teach every side how to love.

The Entertainer

Bloe bloed, gray dust, drifting in the wind,
born in a world of sin.
Old soul, new life begins.
Here before, but I am back again.
Defeated times
after an exhausted storm.
Everyone thought he was gone.
Scream.
Choke.
Pick up the next breath from his last death.
Choose the wicked yet beautiful life's interest
over leaving the soul to rest.
Lesson to test—
it could take millennia to finish or maybe much less.
Destiny knows what's next.
Conquering lands leads others on controversial conquests.
Bless, stop cruel aggressiveness.
Confess the known to the name unknown.
Take care of kids in the home.
World power, language spoken in every zone.
Seven energy exits keep the soul well connected to the universe.
It could be better or worse, horse or hearse.
Net after gross.
Cremation or cold dirt, pain and hurt,
the joys of the world give its true worth.
Despair takes it all away.
C-section or euthanasia determines which day.
In between black and white is gray,
a secure place to stay.
Many people like it that way.

Lightening

You see my light skin.
You probably should call me lightening,
because it's striking the kind of shock I give,
but
you don't
since
you couldn't understand
what I did.
Contemplate
the double-standard ways of life
I live.

Beautifully Dangerous

Resemblances to poisonous species in the jungle didn't push these beautiful creatures toward struggle; rather they were born with it, so they embrace it as if it is part of their muscle. It's the strength to hustle. Everyday life cut through situations with the sharpest knife with ease, these characters can make you believe the most unbelievable in times where everything is extremely critical. Push the mind so hard for the greatest physical. An aesthetic stance with clear intuition creates the appearance that's mythical. This is the dangerous and irresistible.

Blessed till death, with wisdom and intelligence, slide forward with precise elegance. Conquer everything that is wished. Powerful auras engulf the audience. Silence keeps the captivated in suspense. No matter how much the thoughts are blown, it is best to never move the stone. Respect is rewarded to the hard, so, similar to our war soldiers, we never drop our guard. Stand as we are, no matter how high the bar. We're still amongst the stars. Beautiful this, and it's beautiful that. If anyone heard it so much, it could be a fact.

Lustful eyes shade a remarkable disguise, but that extra sense uncovers those lies. Stay ahead, right beside the future, a voice soothing the brain to regroup. Hold back further, then the release of karma sutra. Explosion of truth destroys whoever tries to fool us. Advanced well beyond the average interests, our historical background would raise the eyebrows at the Library of Congress. Moving to the different beat of life, kind of like, but not really the type to just let these experiences completely pass me by. Let these thoughts decide. Then I fly up until it's time to touch down. Don't know what's next, but the thrill is what can be found. Realizations consistently hit the here and now. But how's everything pretty much the same, except for the constant flow of change?

Sexy

Let me tell you a little story about sexy. I keep it sexy. On Mondays, simple is sexy. I ease into the week with it. I keep sexy on a leash. I'm the master of it. It jumps up and down all around me. Sometimes, I have to snatch it back and tell it to calm down. Okay. Sexy! Easy now!

Never Catch Me Desperate

Never catch me desperate. I'll push you deep into debt or get you to place your life up for a bet. You'll go crazy just to forget. Light as a feather, stiff as a board, hands raised up to the heavens, reaching for your Lord. Imagine me eating dirt with only these tears to wash it down. Ruthless stomps put me closer to the earthworms in the ground. Yes, I am designed for success. Standing before me can get you destroyed or blessed. In times of struggle, think about negative and positive schemes. Late bills and an empty fridge will turn into your wildest dreams. Grinning, you're bargaining for easy sinning. I am at the finish line. You can't even make it to the beginning.

Never catch me desperate, because I don't even know how evil I can get. Only God realizes what I'll do to protect. Just in case we keep disaster recovery plans in place, unbeknownst to our enemy to detect at all costs, secrets must be kept. In the flesh, deception and beauty can bring life-and-death regrets or a soul to rest. Nonetheless, bless the best with nothing less. Live your path as close as you can to being fearless. Reckless ways can and eventually will deteriorate good deeds. Internal shock shook the body until it stopped. The brain couldn't believe how much bloed would leave. With it all around the confusion set in. Wasn't sure if it was another birth, an abortion, or death on the skin. Let the body go and the soul stay afloat. Amen.

Conflicts of Interest

Sometimes I wish someone would take me out of this hell, cock the weapon, breathe, then squeeze the trigger and unload that shell. Just embrace the burn, choke down the bleed, hold in the guts, and don't yell. Now let the soul float, because the body is gone. Didn't plan to stay long. These temporary thoughts were going wrong. All I needed was a genuine hug from the one I really loved. I have destroyed many times over and over again. I smiled, picked up the pieces, and glued them back in where I thought they should meet, but look again—the sculpture obviously isn't the same. The cracks run deep. It was your fault. It was mine. I am trying to open my eyes, but am I going blind? I am looking, yet I don't see the signs. I've heard about it before, located in the sixth energy space, called the third eye. Sensing answers to my whys, learning to become wise, strengthen old bonds and cut off loose ties. Species of all kinds swim, sprint, and fly at rates faster than light. Check out my vibe. I am powerful, devised well, quiet, and made to creep, so I can asphyxiate the breath from the fox that simulates the sheep.

Step one, step two, me first, then you. Got the clue. Not all, just a few I loved but had to leave them too. Our life is the jungle, with the cannibals, gorillas, snakes, and other bloedthirsty animals. I kept us moving, pressing hard. I knew up ahead wasn't far. I knew there was more than life on this hazardous floor. I could see above the trees, beyond the canopy, the widespread light, there was no way anyone was fooling me that for twenty-four hours a day it was night. You begged me to slow down, discouraged me from moving on. I smiled back. My intuition sensed something was wrong. I looked around, and before I knew it you were gone. Didn't want you to be left in their hands to die, but I couldn't do anything about it, so for a few moments I stood there and cried. I had to let you go. Whatever happens I may never know. I am alive, and I had to do what I needed to survive.

I really loved you the way my heart knew how. I'm still trying to figure it out, how to make it up to you now. Somewhere along the line, we both got lost in someone else, forgot who we were, how we first met, and lost ourselves. It was good, but how did we forget? All words chosen have been spoken; there's nothing left to be said. Since it didn't work out, I am choosing a sure thing that is sure to prevail. Yes, the sheets are cool. This is it when all else fails. I have all things except for you. That's okay. I still have myself.

Media Scream

Scream from the things I see. Scream from what I watch on
TV. Scream from the content I read. I scream inside from
the pain I've seen in human beings. You see I scream from
here, because they're out of my reach. Scream at the peo-
ple who profit from the proceeds. Scream from evil greed.

I hate evil. I don't hate people. Sometimes I wish the Almighty and
I were equal. It would be a different kind of place—that would be
my earthly promise. We'd know nothing about human trafficking,
pedophiles, rapists, or domestic violence. What does it take to reach
beyond our tolerance? Scream for the bleed that's shed by their inno-
cence. The children—let them grow up without being scarred and
corrupt. What's going through a man's mind that tells him it's okay
to touch? He's allowed to do more to them for less than what he paid
for lunch. I hate these things so much. But maybe what I hate more
is the society that promotes or accepts these children's missed luck. A
different country doesn't make it good. A stated price doesn't mean
someone should and doesn't mean he should rob a child's hood.

Scream from things I see. Scream from what I watch on TV. Scream from
the content I read. I scream inside from the pain I've seen in human be-
ings. You see I scream from here, because they're out of my reach. Scream
at the people who profit from the proceeds. Scream from evil greed.

The already-weak prey on the weak every day of the week. Creeps find
joy in easy defeat. Never challenge anyone around or even me. I could get
you to swallow that dirt beneath your feet. I'm not God, so I can't stop the
whole lot. Now think and stop. Cool down tempers that get hot. Raise
hands up that block—not quick enough to escape the shock. Soft fists and
callous palms create turbulence that shifts until the body rocks and finally
drops. Never faster than the speeding bullet, I couldn't imagine what was
thought many moments before he pulled it. He never left her alone. The

law told him not to go near her job or her home. Sorrow, then stress, lost control. Depression couldn't gauge how low. Took it for granted. Didn't guess her soul would pass over us by tomorrow. A piece of peace, but really the whole piece of peace, is achieved. Those who knew that deeply loved, grieved. Those who didn't know shook their heads in disbelief, then moved onto the next subject to read or changed the channel on TV.

Scream from the things I see. Scream from what I watch on TV. Scream from the content I read. I scream inside from the pain I've seen in human beings. You see I scream from here, because they're out of my reach. Scream at the people who profit from the proceeds. Scream from evil greed.

Violent video games, violent movies, and violent songs—we listen and watch, thus promoting them all. It happens. We assume it must've been something that he saw. No loved one should get that call! What should and what is are obviously two different things. Reality brings awareness of good and evil. Some make it worse, and some make it better for people. Ideas play in a person's mind that could get him away. The crime could've been done better if it was done that or this way. Warning signs are realized that move her that day. Hopelessness to hope clears her mind from his verbal dope. His control over her evaporates into virtual smoke. Donations to centers from the empathic release the choke. The beauty of volunteers dries her tears and covers her like a cashmere coat. So on that note, I can't scream anymore on the inside. I hope awareness will get them out safe and alive so they can thrive. Give sight to the heart that has gone blind. TV shows us what you need. What we read shows us how we can do good deeds— please, so that they're no longer out of my reach. So I don't have to scream from the things I see. Scream from what I watch on TV. Scream from the content I read. I scream inside from the pain I've seen in human beings. I don't want to scream from here, because they're out of my reach, or scream at the people who profit from the proceeds, or even scream from evil greed.

Sleep

Oh, I don't know if I should be telling you this,
deeper in my mind, sharing my business.

I need to let this thing go to get by,
no matter how hard I try.

I can't seem to stay focused during the day.

Please, angels, don't leave me.

God
(Psalms 83:18)

Tell them I need their protection.
I thought my opened Bible was my weapon.

Every day and every night
I need another entity other than myself to win this fight.
I need you to forgive me for not always living right.
Where did the sons of the father go
when I was up against the demons last night?

Ever since I was at least nine
I've always worried about sleeping just fine.

I'm scared to death to go to sleep.
When I do, it's really deep.

A nervous spirit leaving a motionless body—
sometimes it stays, though I wish it didn't.
I close my eyes.
Whoa, something isn't right.
I open my eyes, but I can't see.
The room is too dark.
That's all I can do—
think silent profane screams,
body exhausted without a single move.
Creepy thoughts poison dreams.
It's a frightening rush thrilling a teen.

I haven't gone anywhere. I'm still here.
No voices, just their wicked presence I fear.

I wonder why everybody is fighting to stay alive
when your soul can rest when you die.

Who says you are going to be tormented and burned in hell?
I swear I don't need a straitjacket in a windowless cell.

I'm trying to find out what I sewed that I now reap
just so that I can get some

sleep.

Chapter 4

Ginned

Prayers for Sons

These are my sons.
These are my hons
in the streets,
blowing drugs,
carrying guns.
You know how it is
where we're from,
not dumb,
simply stuck in the present.
I want you alive,
fairy godmother.
I visit you at night,
Queen Hatshepsut, Queen Nefertiti, Queen Elizabeth I,
Queen Cleopatra VII,
reincarnated through and Goddess Isis,
Goddess Lakshmi,
Erzulie, Freda, Dantor, Hanhepi Wi,
all love, wealth, fertility and beauty.
Let our
sons survive.

Bubble World

Blowing bubbles in my bubble world,
don't try to pop my bubbles in my bubble world.
These mean kids have pins
that they're constantly trying to stick in.
It's not just one;
it's a whole bunch of them.
You know the kind
that like to poke his or her finger in your eye
until you turn blind.
Lie and say it was the other guy,
a crap load of bullshit alibis.
Turn the fan on, and watch it all fly.
They're giving it up at any price,
serving the devil with hands on the Bible, hollering,
"Christ."
Who am I to even decide who is living right,
unless they interrupt my life?
Then my words start to take form into a knife,
pierce every part …
Now I'm holding their heart.
These baby whales have nothing on this hungry shark.

Dream Catchers

Dream catchers when they're grinning in a world of sinning. Bet it's worth living. Let me tell you from the beginning. Everything about him flowed just like linen. Early in life he started it in winning. Never two feet on the ground at the same time, he was constantly running. He never gave himself enough time to relax his mind. He kept it locked, loaded, and gunning. Not quite wise, but extremely cunning, always devising a scheme that allowed him to lead the team, chasing those scenes in his dreams. By daylight he was trying to figure out, what did it all mean? Every day and years after, nothing stops progress like a disaster. Not paying attention put him there faster. Reckless and all over the place, nothing is better than that wild taste. And once it's there, only fate can erase it away. Just like it always existed, just couldn't resist it, just as bad as any addiction. Gotta try to have it all. No matter how hard, he will fall. He can't be the one to fault. This is just what he's been taught. He rarely dreamed that he would get caught.

There have been so many others on the passengers' side. No one ever believed. Figured it was another tease. Everyone has these tricks up their sleeves. Never conceived he'd really rise, yet there was this one to give him a try. Even if she'd break down and cry, she'd still give him whatever he requested. Every dream he pitched, she was there to catch it. She held him up like the foundation built above the ground. Keep her around. It was his luck that she was about to fall madly in love. Plus, yes, she's young, beautiful, with no kids. What her parents said, that's what she did. Good girl, but no one knew the secret desires she hid. Like the total opposite way to live. Propped up, listening to the dreams he threw, they both went to bed dreaming of getting rich soon.

So splendid, how he liked to spend it. Like sugar in a bowl, it was very sweet. Every other night she didn't know his plans on keeping her on hold. Just how long would it flow? Only up to the common threshold, and it was too late to let go. Her stomach is constantly tight with fear. She can barely eat, and her thoughts are no longer clear. She just wants him here to keep away the nightmares. Head in the clouds, but don't say it out loud. His future is in doubt. She might care, but she'll take that dare. It's the best bags. It's the clothes with the tags. Botox and cosmetic surgery to tighten what sags. She's older now, but we all still agree she's definitely bad, acquiring everything she wished she had. She'll be dreaming when they come and take everything she thought she had. Nightgown on, no chance for bond in the dark, two hours before dawn. Wet grass pushes her soft knees deep in the earth. Is this what it was all worth? The sacrifices and the hurt? Cold-stone ice cream to a cold-stone holding room? The attorneys will get here soon. All these thoughts will be recounted in a blur. She knew but never envisioned it would actually occur. She kept ignoring that warning she silently heard. She wanted to keep her eyes closed and keep dreaming with him, but this is how it ends. She's left with khaki pants and a shirt from the Federal Bureau of Prisons.

That Chick

I came out of a white girl
the color of raw cocaine
mixed with coca leaves, this and that, and a lot of gasoline.
My last name looks like bloe flame.
Watch how you play.
I easily blow up in the face.
If you keep sniffing me like K-9,
I'ma have you addicted, high, and blind.
They call it love.
I say if they ain't robbing, stealing, cheating,
they ain't had enough.
So what's up? It's like this.
Go ahead and give it up.
Some like it smooth. Some like it rough.
Some like it for a good time. The others go all day and night.
I come in a variety of cuts.
A bit in a bag, I'm the keys in the trunk.
Oh, no,
we don't use keys for our trunks.
What's that smell?
It doesn't smell like skunk.
I'm trying to get myself there safely
to give these people what they want.
We got highway pirates
that rob with masks and a badge;
they keep close watch on the out-of-state tag.
When I get there
they gonna lick me, taste me, rub me on their teeth
till they double see, double say
I'm officially street.
Get live, gangsta certified.

Demand and supply,
they only want the best,
and we all know
we gotta pay more for less.
How many digits can we get
to follow the first one?
We on the run
to get another one
among the numerical and mental confusion.
So fuck the DEA, CIA, FBI,
snooping for a confession
We don't have none.

The Feds and Effects

It's human instinct to watch out for one's own interest, and it's so easy to forget what could happen next. Everything is touched from what we digest, right down to how we conduct our business. It might be this. Don't lose sight of the rest. This game in life is a constant test. Every move comes with consequences. We want the most but end up with so much stress. There are many perspectives to this mess. What I do in life isn't always about me getting ahead. It started with us. Let me just introduce you to the Feds and a ghetto classic.

Marquis Black came up hard and way below broke, living amongst thrown trash, cracked concrete, and dirt. He thinks that this life has only three hopes: death, chains, and dope. Anyone who's ever suffered from hunger knows that it's not a joke. Backed in the corner and nothing to eat, this man turns to the streets. Mr. Black is a hood success by the age of eighteen. He buys everything beyond one's wildest dreams. His clients are fiends. He's a fiend for that green. Yes, he's been through much and has come extremely far. Mr. Black is at the top and in charge. It's all good till the Feds pick up George. He's a rat, and you know it all after that. Here are the facts: It's not just him in this domino effect. Everyone in this system is affected. The family hurts now, because he isn't around. The kids don't have anyone to look up to, so they look down. The banks, mortgage companies, and stores take the shock of it all. Look at the economy fall. With less money, there's more debt. Everyone's mixed up in it. No one's paperwork is consistent. Scam after scam is exposed fraudulent. Before they're paid, the money is spent. What I don't get is how people will try to keep up with someone they never met. It's not known what's in those pockets. The bank accounts look like tennis courts in the projects. Back and forth, checks bouncing through fabric-less nets. Let us guess, the Feds are going to take care of all of this, not without charging us multiple amounts of interest.

That's what we get, less than what we started out with.

Greatest Gift to the Mistress

Freedom is everything. I took it all.
I knew your flaws. I got the best years of your life and touched your wife.
I raised your kids. I spent your money, controlled the way you lived.
You did all this for me. I only gave you a bid.

I stayed at your house. I threw all that you called sacred "out."
I kept your mind in doubt.

You broke up and sold concrete on the street.
Money would get you to see me faithfully in a week.
Ever read Donald Goines's *Dopefiend*?
I'd have you do anything for me.
They sacrifice all intangible assets on the altar for yours truly.

I love to sit back and watch what you like to do,
how you move on top. Your vibe is so cool.

A couch potato, a moviegoer, I am in the scene.
I'm dirty, but then again I am so clean.

I just might be you. A body only houses one soul,
so just where do you go?
I don't know, and I don't care.
Um, you can go over there,
but you got to get the _ _ _ _ out of here.

I always knew you were so generous,
the way you showered gifts on the ones you loved.
You better not dare put anyone other than me above.

You were mine the first time we kissed.
I could've been what was wet on your lips when you took a sip.
I was the Dom, the Krug Rose, Louis, the Cris.
Only one swallow guaranteed my entrance.
I brought you two seconds of bliss on earth's timescale.
I kept you on the track. You got slick.
I took you off the rail.
That's how I bit back.

The game you choose. Players choose to lose.
Commitment-less, I don't stress these fools.
I just use them like tools.
Pages keep turning. I am the mistress.
I can't lose.

I set up the game. The inventor makes the rules,
designed for those who don't have anything else to do.
Clueless. Ahh … I get to decide for you.

General power of attorney for the brain dead,
I am the head of the Fed.

Controlling inflation in the streets and how money gets in and out,
you better believe I know when, why, and where there's a drought.

I have eight queens ready on the front lawn.
They only move forward to act like a pawn.
Surprise attacks had you shaken at dawn.

This is the climax of the story today.
I took your freedom away,
thought you could pay.
Thanks, but the money is mine already.
Remember
I was printing it in Washington
at the US Treasury.

Now make some cents.
Better yet, I have something to give for such a wonderful gift:
twenty years to life—how's that for a legal bid?

Him

How can you dare even think to leave me gasping for oxygen like this?
They saw what I didn't see:
the DNR (do not resuscitate) flyer on the wall.
You were checking out my energy.
The attention smoothed out what made my skin crawl.
My temple here stands with passion.
Infatuation lost to love stops the lungs from collapsing.
Keep the body moving.
Listen to you so much.
I became what I thought of you.
I'm overdosing and sick as the flu.
Yet, I keep denying myself this truth.
That fact that we are done with each other—we're still not through.
What am I going to do?
The relationship is intense and critical.
I'm scared to death.
I could be losing this bet.
Could've sworn I would win this test.
My vision is cloudy, and I must be going blind.
In time, your anesthesia has my body numb.
Through the cataracts I can see you holding something
bloedy and pumping.
Please,
hold it carefully and put it back in my chest.
I don't want to go into cardiac arrest.

Ex Fool

I've done it all.
I'm guilty as charged.
None of that counts
since I didn't get caught.
Evidence deleted, hidden, or lost,
best story bought,
fought to exhaust,
suspicions and allegations—
their intuition is always off.
By the time they get close
I'm gone.
Holding the world in your palms
could seem so small
when you are used to carrying all of the galaxies in your arms.
These minute problems solved,
look around—I got a cause.
I'm empty if you're not involved.
Now I'm a fool for you.
I forget how to think
and wait till you tell me what to do.
I ain't got a clue.
Your ways seem better than what I knew.
My ex?
I don't remember who.
You've been away.
It's a long time overdue.
What I gotta say,
I waited so long for this day.
I needed to be your date.
Eventually you showed up,
but you were too late.

I've suffered aneurysms, tears, and heartbreak.
Something changed.
Almost strange,
Ironic to see fate
laughing in our face.
I'm simply amazed
at the fact
my emotions are no longer fazed.

Mighty Powers

People and their memories,
bipolar switch from happy to angry,
tied up, focusing on dead deeds.
Aggressors always screaming,
"Let it fucking go!"
Victims seem to have the past in a choke hold.
Okay, hop in a balloon and fly where the wind blows.
I've got scars below my knees and above my elbows,
plus a warning that breezes lightly in my earlobe,
paying attention to what lies beneath the surface.
I'm the calmest when everybody else is nervous.
I'm as guarded as the president, with his bullet-
proof vehicles and his secret service.
I've got people who will kill,
people who will block and use their bodies to shield,
to make sure not one drop of my own bloed will spill,
who listen and care about how I feel.
We bond to seal unspoken deals.
More plastic surgery than most you know,
and
I'm still real.
Some are on weird drugs and laced reefer.
I'd rather float under general anesthesia.
Take a break from the world for a couple hours.
It's the doctor and God, with all their mighty powers,
more perfection to keep the envious sour.
I've got them looking at me like the sun above all glass towers.
The ugliest shit makes the most beautiful flower.
Superior to the inferior,
I devour cowards.

Idolism

Praise the mortal gods.
We're practicing idolism.
My brain has been robbed.
Drop dead when he stopped.
I'm floating amidst a cloudy mental prison.
Choose to remain spiritual.
I can't deal with religion,
skipping along the funny farm,
licking on temp tattoos on my salty arm,

crickets jumping and birdies whistling
between the on-and-off-again drizzling.

Inhale the pastel grass,
bending in the breeze.
Turquoise bubble glass, bees in the trees,
coloring the sun green
are what I see.
Lots of kisses and smiles on my body—
okay, it's true. I'm constantly caught in a sunny daydream
just to get away from the jealous screams.

I'll do almost anything to escape the truth,
like Americans counting coups,
each one paying for a bowl of soup and a whore in a saloon,
too ugly to deal with the pain.

I hot-wire his heart,
get on a plane, and go very far,
and if
I could breathe there
I'd be on my way to Mars.
Soon realize it's too cold and too dark.

I'd be all alone,
so I'd hurry up and come home
to a life that's not that bad.

When out there exist horrible nightmares
of people who pretend but don't really care,
makes me super scared.
It could cause the soul to break and dissipate,
like it was never there.
Each time I swear
we were a good pair,
but by the following of every year,
my memory of them is cleared.

Chapter 5

Storms and Thorns

A Thought

I wait to feel the wetness from your kiss.
I only taste the saltiness from tears on my lips.

The lump in my throat makes it hard to swallow.
The weight I lose should make me look like a runway model.
Imagine me as a chocolate Easter bunny,
all dark and hollow.
I could pretend that it doesn't mean anything,
whether I see you today or tomorrow.
There lays my sorrow.
Even the slightest mark of rejection is horror.

What I wish puts me in the midst of what does not exist,
similar to this,
mansions in the projects.
If I never saw you again,
I wonder what would be the strength of its effect.
Would all of the thoughts storm in
past events,
or would it be like extinct animals with not one left?

The Sin

If I could take out my heart from my chest, I would place it somewhere
no one could guess. At best I'd let this mind forget all those regrets.
Pretend like it never existed and place those thoughts in a box of deaths.
Shake off the tears and let the alcohol sanitize the fears. After all that
rain, there should be some sun. You'd think I should be done, as if I
didn't notice the thief in my temple with the gun, or that I'm not the
only one. He smiled, and I adored his face. As he spoke, I enjoyed every
word while swallowing the taste. Out of my own selfishness—and that
is the real reason I understand—I just did it for the thrill of conquer-
ing my own plan. The mind plays such a tricky part. It still has its ways
of manipulating the heart. Blame it on the eyes for letting in the lies.
Believe half of what I see and nothing of what I hear. So now my eyes
blame it on my ears for not shutting out what was clear. I wanted to love.
I wanted to trust. I just wanted it to be us. It was just lust. I could be-
lieve I'm infatuated with all my heart. My heart doesn't send the same
signals to the north like it used to, but the south has betrayed her too.
The heat and excitement have turned cool. He was so funny, the way he
carried on and joked. I was foolish and filled with some kind of hope.
It must've been a vampire that sunk his teeth into my neck, because he
left a mark on me I doubt I'll forget. I couldn't resist his charms. It went
out of control when I was in his arms. I really can't remember the others
anymore. Life is different from before, like the rich forgetting the days
they were poor. The gears shift so fast that when it cracks it's hard to get
back to the right way to react. I'm starting to believe that it's all falling
apart, since I'm encased in a body and not a machine. I won't fall to pieces
if you know what I mean. It's just a little scratch that left a light scar.
Still trying to figure out how I fell so hard, how I let down my guard.
It had to have been when I let him go deep within. That was the sin.

The sin is going against your own intuition—knowing you should leave,
but staying instead, falling behind when we can get further ahead.

Go ahead with your plans. I don't need you to be my man. I understand you can. I won't put up with these demands you love. I don't give a damn. I am who I am. You are who you are. We're both superstars. We wouldn't have it any other way. Great attracts great. Great also will push it away, like Brussels sprouts on my plate. Breakups I hate, so I let them linger till they fade. Two kids in the sandbox. I'm glad we played. We came out dirty and learned from our mistakes. Time—I guess that's what it all takes to ease the heartache.

Granted: Her vs Him

Her:

I took you for granted for so long until you couldn't stand it. What pushed
you so far? There's so much that's made us hard. Arguments at these
bars—regurgitated secrets put me back on guard. Covered deceptions
have put us in the middle of war, stepping on granite floors. It's never
enough; we're always searching for more. Body scrubs surrounded by
candles around the tub—swear it to anyone in the moment that it's love.
But what? The feelings disappear as the euphoria dies down. I used to
always want you around, yet these ugly realizations start to become clear.
As soon as it's all over, I don't want you near. Or do I think this because
I know you'll always be here? Giving in to every whim was the great-
ness to the beginning. So new and so fresh, it seems that we never forget
what we thought was the best, or was it that we were simply a wanted
guest? Breakfast in bed right after sex, just before you left, still no regrets.
Time after time, with it so far behind, we're stuck in rewind, not moving
on with our lives. It's supposed to get better. I really wish that it was.

They always say that they care. I guess he really does. Never expected
to change those wonderful days. Never expected to see either one of our
tarnished ways. Don't know where we're going, like a rat in a maze. The
candles that were burning are almost touching the wick. Just like the
wax, we're ceasing to exist. The ambitions we had, so different, it's sad.
I'm trying to understand the reason we crossed paths. Through the bit-
terness, I'm glad we can still find a laugh. The rains in the clouds, I'm
about to throw in the towel. Come over here and remind me of the way
it used to be done, the youth, and the fun. It was us and the sun. The
problems we have could be so easily solved by repairing the damage we
have mentally caused. The disrespect and the names, the manipulative
games—it won't ever change, at least not until we can relate. We take ev-
erything for granted until we see it's all stopped, confused and wondering.
Just when were we robbed of the passion and heat, the excitement of it

all, the innocent curiosity and seeing no flaws, so interested in the other we'd wait for that call? So sweet before, we've gotten so raw. No matter the situation, the bills were always paid. Your word was your honor, and you know that's why I stayed. That's all well and good, but how much can I take? See that money you gave I still could've made. Not said out of hate but to note my own faith. I take it for granted you'll always stay with me, but don't take it for granted that I won't just up and leave.

Him:

Ok, baby, sup? Looks like my time is up. I've been listening to what you've been saying. Yup, you've changed. You've got your own thing going on now, huh? I guess you got tired of me checking your phone. Figured out you activated the passcode lock and silenced the ringtone. Got me wondering what you been hiding. We started arguing and fighting, probably what you like, because you got an excuse to not give me any action. You think I'm dumb. I can see the way you're reacting, that you're covering something. The vibe wasn't right. Nobody's getting any sleep tonight. Put all my money down in the bank that your boy is right. Guess I didn't have to party that way. Maybe I shouldn't have lived so far away. But, baby, just stay. Even though it wasn't perfect, I've done plenty for you. Girl, I don't deserve this. Can't believe you're really leaving. I'm a little nervous. No, I don't wanna let you go. It's gotta be the way you put it down on me, make me forget I was acting crazy. Got my brain all mixed up, confused. Had to let you know I'm no fool!

Her:

Look at how long I've stayed to see if it will change, erase the past that caused the heartache. In transition to the very next stage—after all of that, it's gotta be great. Take those as lessons and never mistakes. If we choose faith, we can say it's never too late. Make the decision to change on that very date. Much better than back then, I gotta confess. It was so constant. I'd thought it would never end—the money, the lifestyle, the plans with these friends. The actress in the movie lives in the moment right in front of the video lens. Never thought I can't. Always knew I can. Believe in myself. Just wasn't sure of these men. With or without him, I was aware that I can't remove every single problem. Being single won't necessarily solve them. What's been said before has been said again. It looks like the directors are ready for some action. Deceptions can get extremely taxing. Lie after lie—like the stars, they light up the eyes. Something you can see, but way out of your reach. Think of me, because these days we rarely speak. A lot of time went by. You know how hard I tried. I barely recognized you when you opened the door. This won't work anymore. I marched right past you on those granite floors.

No Conversation

I fell in love
still down.
Floating high in the sky for you,
feeling like
an astronaut skipping on the moon.
All these chicks fighting for your attention,
but if you keep ignoring me,
I'm putting you on suspension.
I don't want the conversation.
I want passion and penetration,
sweat, kissing, and squeezing.
The way you look at me,
I understand what you're saying.
I don't give a damn about the others you've been dating.
I do things to you
that get the bloed pumping, keep your heartbeat racing.
Vice versa from those good beatings I've taken.
Thought I forgot about you
till I woke up,
saw no text,
and
realized I'm still waiting.

Face-to-Face

What would I say to you
face-to-face?
It's been ages. I'm wondering
if I would feel the same
dead asleep but still managed to answer my phone.
That excitement I used to experience when we were alone—
skip of my heartbeats,
the nervous words I tend to speak,
too many thoughts of what, where, how, why, when, who.
I know I won't say anything
(scoff).
I know I would just look
deep inside.
I'm like rubble crumbling down a mountainside.
I know I would just look
at a face I haven't seen face-to-face in so long—
your face, your beautiful face.
I remember the late nights and the early days,
back cracking, breaking dawns,
the smile and your eyes looking back at mine.
No one could ever replace
one of a kind. Oh,
I think you can see me start to fall.
Is that why you're hugging me?
Can't bear it all.
You've got me up against the wall.
I can't move one inch,
weak and paranoid, out of control.
I'm afraid you saw,
and then you let go.
No!

You're doing it again,
turning your back on your friend.
Tell me this ain't a habit.
Tell me it's a trend.
Getting a text, hearing your voice, seeing your face is the attention,
prescription of my medicine.
If you stop,
we both have lost a battle
that we fought long and hard
face-to-face.
I wanna hold your face in my palms,
following them down your arms
till I hold your hands in my palms.
I'd do this face-to-face,
but you've been gone,
baby, oh my baby, very long.

The Dirty Truth

When I stomped out his life,
it shook the earth.
I have no idea how bad he hurts.
Does he hurt?
Well, he gets what he deserves,
pretending to be a blessing covering a curse.
The friendliest kind can do the worst,
kissing and hugging you with bombs in their shirts.
Smiles behind green is where they lurk,
alligators and crocodiles in the murk.
I wouldn't beware.
I let him take me there.
Trusting the devil will always be a lie.
Without the truth the soul starts to die.
I gave him what he liked.
I gave him an exciting life.
Now that it's over,
I wanna bury this bloedy knife.
The one I pulled from my pelvic bone
he stabbed me with.
We could've had kids,
but look at what we did,
some things against each other.
We both couldn't handle it.

When He Took Off His Ring

Hello, my good ole friend. It's been some time since I've seen that wonderful grin. Nothing in the world felt as good as hugging him. Maybe he didn't care or thought I didn't notice what I saw happening, as he got more comfortable, what was on his mind. I couldn't tell. He kicked off his shoes, loosened his belt, undressed all the way down to his boxer shorts. Never went to court. His wife hadn't heard of the bad news. When he took off his ring… He wasn't married anymore. So don't go blaming me when he did that. He looked like he was free when he took off his ring.

He wasn't married anymore.

Now life is hard enough. No one has the right to judge. Maybe he just needed some love from his good ole friend who was as happy as back then, understand as best she can, knew that life wasn't perfect. She would never home wreck. She never wanted to steal him from his wife, but would borrow him every now and then at night. Then again when he took off his ring, he wasn't married anymore. So don't go blaming me when he did that. He looked like he was free when he took off his ring.

He wasn't married anymore.

The hours have passed, and we've shared some of the best times in our lives within these walls. We have nothing to hide. Would never regret being in his arms. The birds are chirping, and it's past dawn. There goes the alarm. He gets up and uses his toothbrush I've set aside, puts back on his shoes, tightens his belt on his pants, smiles one last time, and slides back on that ring he took off last night. He's married now, and we hug and kiss each other as good ole friends do. I close the door behind me without any shame, because when he took off his ring, he wasn't married anymore. So don't go blaming me when he did that. He looked like he was free when he took off his ring.

He wasn't married anymore.

Get 'Em, Miss 'Em, Forget 'Em

We were cool from the very start.
We knew the game. We used to peek at each other's cards.

We were on the same team. I would recount stories.
I'd watch you begin to daydream.

I could tell you wished it was yourself. I'd brush it off and remind myself.

This guy knows we're only friends.
Don't get it confused. If we get together, we know the negligence.

We told the lies, did the cheating, the pimping, the abuse,
but we keep smiling, touching, talking, and we choose.
We wanna know what it's like to be with-
out the other two—your girl, my ex, dude.
Scrambled, shaken, tossed up, the winner is only
gonna be one of us. You think it's you.

I say I've had better luck. You ain't never been in love till you got stuck.

Thinking I'm tripping,

boy, you still don't know you've stumbled and fallen, holding.
I got that ... all in.

I get down with something them girls don't got. When that door locks,
I'm turning you inside out like dirty socks. I give you electric shocks.
Is there some kind of mental block? I don't understand how you for-
got how I take you through the roof, slide down, and land on top. I'm
missing you so much. I wish these stupid feelings would just *stop*.

If someone mentions your name, I might remem-
ber ... sometime, somewhere around that day, okay.
I thought you were solid. Why'd you give me the gold plate?

In fantasy it's all symbolic, almost like yesterday. The reality ...
you couldn't keep it straight. I don't need anyone to remind me,
so let's keep it that way.
I let your memory fade.

Red Line

I'm really busy,
but not too busy to know you haven't called.
I look at the time and date on my watch—
it's been days.
What keeps you so swamped?
That's not it at all.
Nothing's wrong with me.
I'm not being that clingy.
You're just married. You're married with a family.
That's not my responsibility.
That's your interest.
I don't want to be involved.
You see the way it goes. You should know
I don't have a problem to fault.
We can't be together.
We were in the moment.
Those wild nights I recall.
I get you have to go.
Well, so do I.
I can't keep a man who cheats on his wife.
What a life of lies!
I respect honesty.
You do some things I despise.
I don't care.
You're not mine.
Anything with gloss can shine.
It's only the best that can move through time.
When it comes to love,
I'm only half blind.
Red flags shoot up in me like a stop sign,
so I check out deader than a flat line.

Soul Shock

My organs are
crashing in.
My house is burning down.
The past is lost. The present …
Pause.
Wait a minute now.
Our future's gone!
You can't tell,
because I'm sitting calm.
Deep inside
Hurricane Pick-a-Name is going on.
Bloed splashing, veins cracking, cells collapsing,
a twisted storm.
Take a moment to see
the devastating reality
ripping left to right, tearing up everything that's out of sight.
Praise me.
I smile one so bright
for covering up
every disaster
that's rocked my life.

Transformation

Damn love.
It gives me pain I know I don't deserve.
Damn lies.
I'd rather hear the truth of silence than those words,
something I haven't heard.
Damn you.
You get on my nerves, but don't go …

Captain of the vessel fell asleep.
Pirate of the sea, take over my ship.
With guns and swords, come steal the reward—
chest full of jewels, barrels of whiskey to sip,
bloed, guts, and body parts,
the stench of mud paste.
I don't recognize your face,
taking over the best booty you ever hit,
oars thrown overboard.
Everyone else is long gone in the mist.
I'm sinking down to the ocean floor.
Every bit of me is covered and wet.
Not an inch of me can be seen.
I'm reappearing with the most beautiful creatures to stay clean.
I was once on top of constant turmoil and abuse.
Now, I'm at the bottom in harmony with the ele-
gant and rich, floating where they choose.

Dream Sounds

I looked so crazy today.
I tripped and fell to the ground.
I remember I was walking along.
I was living my life
with my music turned up,
but I couldn't hear a sound.
And then you came singing this song.
I never heard it before.
The past faded out till I couldn't hear it anymore.
My ears were picking up on the richest symphony
that couldn't be ignored.
You gave me a little more.
You started showing me a dream.
The colors were bright and glowing in the scene.
We were laughing, smiling, and everything.
Out of nowhere, it was pitch-black.
I was back
in my room by myself.
I tried to close my eyes to go where we were.
It was too late.
I was awake.

Heart Island

I'm earthquaking
right down the middle. I'm shaking.
The ground is breaking,
splitting the world apart, Mother Nature's broken heart.
Will I sink to the bottom for the fish to live in
or turn into an island
where the future takes its vacation?
These roots shoot up and keep racing.
I'm out of here. I'm done waiting.
Drift into the ocean. All these waves of emotion
are making me seasick. Keep going till I settle on where to live.
I see volcanoes in the midst. I don't stop till
I reach mountains that are high,
the perfect place for me and the sun to kiss.
We can have kids,
make babies of coconut trees,
grow mangoes and juicy pineapples for the peo-
ple who stood with me to eat.
Sometimes a heartbreak is what we need
to become beautiful for the world to see.

Bloed on the Sand

I think of the days when we were so sweet and
fresh as the day a love child is born,
not these times when we are battered and worn.
What were the words that were sworn?
I'll keep away the clouds, rain, and storms,
give you roses minus the thorns,
bring you nothing but gold and rainbows,
lots of highs, no lies, no lows.
The days passed into the morrows.
In too deep, the joy slipped into sorrows,
engorged from the tsunami I swallowed.
Events have turned me into a different woman,
flowers with thorns forced in my hands.
There's bloed on the sand.
None of this was my original plan.
When you let me go, I should've never come back when I ran.
You're not quite the man.
Damn, I gotta try it all over again.

Mad

I was mad … mad at some things you did to me in the past. I
was mad at the fact and had to get you back. Yes, I was bad, but
it felt good to see how you'd react. You were mad. That's why
you treated me like that. Never-ending cycle—it's tit for tat.

Been with me for years, watched me go out of my way, talked to me ev-
ery day, knew I was alone most of the time. You had your own agenda:
getting drunk with your friends in other cities, following chicks on
social media with big booties and titties. How can strangers, football
players, and employees get more loyalty, nonstop playing poker and
war games? You've been acting iffy—DUIs and telling lies, not mak-
ing it in till daylight. Don't know everything going through your brain.
I only knew you were taking too much time, bringing me regret and
shame. You had a way of making me feel sick inside, so I got fed up,
took control of my life, made some decisions of my own. You keep call-
ing. I'm not answering the phone. I'm in interesting places with famous
faces in different time zones. That's better than arguing with you in
my bedroom. You begged to know, so I told you so. Revenge is cold,
but only if the victim burns. You never stopped tripping, never let it
go. I guess you were mad. You were mad … mad at some things I did
to you in the past. You were mad at the fact and had to get me back.
Yes, you were bad, but it felt good to see how I'd react. I was mad.
That's why I treated you like that. Never-ending cycle—it's tit for tat.

Been with you for years. Been through the good times and tears. Been
with me through the laughs and the crazy rants. Been through so much.
I can't … I can't keep giving you another chance. I'm overwhelmed
that you don't understand. I tried to explain, but it's clear you're stuck
in some ways. It's full drama on stage that constantly plays. Principles
and chemistry—our balance has tipped off the scales. Respect and
passion are not doing too well. I'm irritated and bored. We're both an-
noyed. I've gotten tired of blaming and profane renaming. No more

nagging, no more complaining. I'm forgiving and letting go of the hat-ing. Going through it all made me mad. I was mad ... mad at some things you did to me in the past. I was mad at the fact and had to get you back. Yes, I was bad, but it felt good to see how you'd react. You were mad. That's why you treated me like that. Now I'm ending the cycle, switching up my act, leaving the past in the past. I'm done with that.

Bad Girls Don't Get the Bloes

If I say no sex, should I stop the texts?
I thought we were friends.
Silence …
The best mysteries come from the most twisted suspense.
Turned off, turn on.
Your voice is my favorite song.
My mind is lost. I'm prepared to leave.
Then I think back. I forgot my keys.
You hold them by rationing out what I need.
I thought I was being reasonable, or is it greed?
Is wanting it all such a bad thing?
She can keep the band. I want the earrings.
She can clean your home. I'm trying to get my own.
In different country codes, drinking so much champagne,
the pretty waitresses keep it cold.
She's at home, spreading the ketchup on the
meat loaf with a side of mustard.
I'm at the Lobster Bar, eating lamb chops and lemon custard.
She can keep what she has. I'd rather stay happy being bad.

Bad girls don't get the bloes. We're on the move, doing what we wanna do.
No more heartbreaks.
We don't cry. Luxury apartment in the high-rise,
all glass ocean views and city lights.

Do you criticize?
I live the life you might fantasize.
Call me what you want.
I'll have as many boyfriends as I like.
I am single and uncommitted
I fall in the moment every minute.

I enjoy peace, and sometimes I like some company
with the guys, the girls, or my family.
I am independent, stay busy, and work hard to stay fit.
Open up the fridge—
everything reads natural and organic,
same with the pantry.
I practice Duolingo every day,
a little Spanish to order in Latin restaurants on
the Islands or in the United States,
French for when I visit Paris to dine and shop,
Portuguese in Brazilian thongs to tan without a top.
Everybody else can keep what they have.
I'd rather stay happy being bad.

Marathon

Men in my past remind me of dirt swept off the porch after a rainstorm,
washed up and gone …
Really now, come on.
Do snakes have ears?
I survive off of sensing what is clear.
What could I be doing wrong?
We get along,
but how can the queen of the game keep get-
ting played by these rooks, crooks, and pawns?
If he were king,
he'd know not to leave me too long
or
too far from his body and arms.
Up all night,
without a wink of sleep until way past dawn.
Champions keep coming,
but
not
one
has
won
this
marathon.

Part 2

Wrinkled Sheets

The Love Inspired Intellectual Property
of the Gordona Bloe Collection.

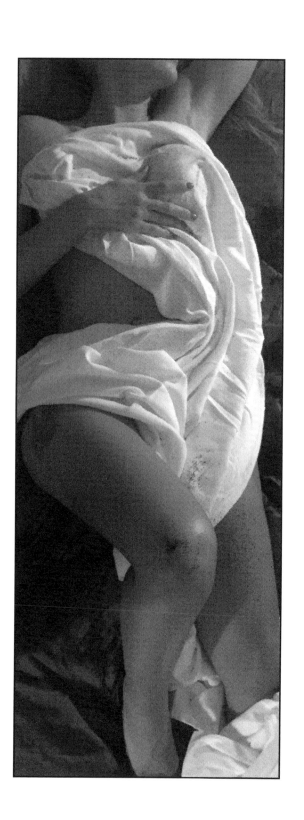

Daredevil

Come on, baby.
I see the looks you're shooting me.
Welcome to the side of being carefree.
Tired of being an angel since you were a child,
always in line like going to lunch in single file.
Ain't nothing like beautiful teeth and a stunning smile,
a mind that reads books by the pile,
a body like yours that runs lots of miles.
You're so busy.
You've got me going wild.
I know it's been a while.
Time to be a daredevil.
Honey, I've got the cape.
I'll make sure you'll be very safe.
Jump on my back. Let's go anywhere you name.
The world's got you locked up in a cage.
Break free, and live to change.
You would've died if I never came.
I rescued you from a life of lames.
Come on, girl. Your style will never be the same.
Pinpoint anyone who tries to play games.
Throw away the umbrella, and let it rain.
There's sunshine above the clouds that dries up the pain.
You've been wishing for this day.
Now is the time. Don't let the opportunity get away.
My little daredevil, you're thinking too hard, try-
ing to be careful. Let it go. Let's go.
Think of this.
Everybody else—they just
wish, wish, wish,
wish they had enough guts to get up and leave like this.

My sweet little daredevil,
they're gonna be sick
when they see what you came back with,
all those things from your shopping trips—
room service, parties around the world, drunk
off of too many champagne sips,
woozy from each other's lips.
Falling in love is like opening up your arms and jumping off a cliff.
I'm beneath your body. You can feel me shift.
Aerodynamics keep us steady in the wind.
I got you,
my little daredevil.
You're thinking too hard, trying to be careful. Let it go. Let's go.
Daredevils behind their desks, daredevils in college finishing up their test,
daredevil models looking their best, daredevils sin and confess,
look great in nothing less.
Daredevils don't let me rest.

Papa Passion

Hey, Papa Papa. Hay's for horses. Built like one. Got a shotgun. Merking mommies, putting bullets in, grazing lungs. Wow, gorilla love. But I'm your sweet and precious. Let's go home. Ready for breakfast. Legs around your neck, gold rope necklace, really get to it, build up an appetite. Plenty of meat to nibble, lick, and bite. I'm sexy. I'm guilty. My ways in the bedroom are filthy. The color's honey. The texture's silky. I ease down light. I am the hype. No need to say. I know what you like. I'm your fantasy tonight.

Welcome to the Brazilian Steakhouse, land of the cannibals. I love me a Hannibal. How do you like your meat? Cut yourself a piece. Go deep, till I can't stand no more, face almost hitting the floor, ranting all kinds of nasty things, pushing my back against the door. Get your iron levels up, color of a sugar cookie. Neither one of us is a rookie, skipping the gym today just to play hooky, sweating it out now, bent in different positions around the couch. Ahhh, ohhh, and ouch! That's how we do it. Break, move it. Turn up the music. Go ahead and knock it out, anywhere in the house. I'm down. That's what I'm about. Papa Papa, ain't no doubt. We got it going on. This is the recipe for some exotic kids, so it goes like this: Shake it up a bit. Light-skinned women and dark-skinned men, been in. Dark-skinned women and light-skinned men, it's a beautiful thing, like the stars kissing heaven. I call this my Papa Passion.

We got babies to make. Throw your organic sugar on my flour and eggs, mix it up, and let it bake. This is really special. God doesn't make mistakes. Put your mouth on my neck, and sink your teeth in. I'm floating off the weed and gin. If this is wrong, forgive me, because I love to sin. Slapping my ass is like throwing the bass in. You're killing it tonight. I can't stop grinning. By tomorrow morning I'll be notifying my next of kin. All this time I'm wondering, *Goddamn, where have you been?*

Various Rewards

Put your diamond-cut, black mamba in my creamy, smooth, rose-gold skin. You light up my universe, pushing up against my G-nerve. I'll give you the best. The best is what you deserve. You can squeeze my curves. Let's do what we do till we're done. This is not a rerun; it's a sexy starting sensation. I like your mind. I respect how you live and think. Like gadgets that link, we sync. You are a smart guy. I too am bright and fly. Let's take a ride to the beach and watch the waves roll in with the tide. Place your hands on my leg, where the sun is warming my thigh. We're not saying anything; we're listening to the birds sing. I am looking like your queen. You are looking like my king.

I only accept bars of gold in my federal reserve. Haven't you heard investments are shooting up the way I conserve? It's the only bank you can trust. All the others can look, but they can't touch. Imagine what these frauds show. I can see it from a distance, you know—scams, bad business plans, and bonds that fold. I keep the best on hold. My security's tight, lock and load. Giddyap, my man's so dope. Watch how we flow. We're both sexier than the status quo. Don't park your ass over here. You will get booted and towed. Look at you go. Don't gotta see you no more. Sent you all the way to your car door, set up proper couture from the top of my head to my feet on the floor. To my left is my papa. Mama adore. We leave the club at a quarter to four. I've been drinking. He can hit it till he gets sore. I'm too numb to feel anymore. We're at my place in the loft. I do what he says and take it off. I don't have a cold, yet when he smacks that from the back, I start to cough. Trying to get a grip on the headboard, I'm dying a wonderful death at the hand of his ninja sword. Don't stop now. Keep stabbing me some more. I'm praising him like he's the good Lord. He's the priest. I'm the nun, the way he takes me to church. We take communion. We're each other's refreshments. He gives me grape juice, and I give him toast till we both catch the Holy Ghost. Whoa!

God damn, I gotta express. You're sexy as a panther moving toward the kill, calculating every move of the deal, analyzing the players in this game of chess is real, way ahead of what's next, but not missing a step—perfect and precise silence. You're working with extreme intuitional guidance, so powerful and dangerous yet beautiful in the same breath. The prey will stop breathing and get crushed to death, shocked by the hot, piercing grip. She's being eaten alive in his mouth, and she's slowing, sliding down inside. Each part of her feels his tongue, tasting her flesh, satisfied and content. He licks lips, then thinks to himself she was delicious. She's been completely consumed and now a part of him. For her, that's the end. By tomorrow he'll be doing it all over again.

You could be my dangerous habit. It's the life of reward and consequences. I wanna submit under your grip. I don't care. The surprise is worth the risk. No one ever said life was fair. I'll take my chances. That's the way to live. It's the life of reward and consequences.

Chief Angel

So many stars in my sheets,
call me
the American flag—
red, white, and royal bloe.
Pledge allegiance to me.
I'm back,
as a matter of fact.
How is that? I ain't bad.
I am a Nefertiti classic.
I got these heretical kings going mad.
Raised to the top,
you know what to do, like you always knew.
Tell the truth.
You've never been this high.
They say it's extremely hard to try,
asking if it's a hurricane outside.
It's Sande.
When I raise up and fly,
rather be quiet than lie about what I did in life
more than twice, and it's nice. Then he's mine … till I die.
Smooth honeyed days and hot sticky nights,
wicked ways and sharp bites.
I'm swimming in the sea with the sharks tonight.
My archangel has flown down to my side.
Chief Angel,
I respect
how you guide and protect.
I submit under your finesse.
My mind is blown from your effects.
Everybody else thought I was too complex.
How did you know?
How did you guess
what I needed next?

Up Close and Personal

I wasn't sure how you would be in real life. Didn't know at the time if I was your type. We've seen each other out and about every now and then, sometimes by ourselves and sometimes with our friends. Then it happened. When I met you, you were everything I like in a person. Mmmm … all up close and personal. It was like a magnetic pull. I was drawn to you. No more obstacles existing between us. I am the one you can trust. I am the one you can love. You wanted to know what took me so long to get to you. I wanted you to make the first move. Finally, the moment and place were right. All this time brought us to this day. I realize you were too far away.

Let me say what I gotta say. We're adults, and we don't have to play those immature games. Don't expect me to change. Baby, I'll make sure it only gets better. We'll be smiling so much. We'll be light as a feather. Peanut butter and toffee crunch, we go good together. There's no one who has anything close to your style. If you want, here's my number to dial. Your appeal is out of this world to me. Mmmm … I like you up close and personal. It was like a magnetic pull. I was drawn to you. Rubbing on my back and being affectionate, respecting my mind and listening—just those little things are what make you the best.

I'm bursting inside with stars and hearts. Something beautiful is taking charge. I'm beginning to let down my guard. I think I'm in love. Since you, that's what I've found. I'm convinced by now that's what I'm made of lately. I haven't felt as rough, like everything's okay. I can handle all this stuff. I won't say anything, I think to myself. I'm not quite ready to go out on the limb. I don't want to scare him. I used to be hard. You've made me mushy soft again, kind of like the first time, as if I'm swirling around in the atmosphere. This feeling to me is so rare. We might make a great pair. In the meantime, come over here, or I can come over there. Either way, I don't care, just as long as we're up close and personal. It's like a magnetic pull. I'm drawn to you.

Boy Crazy Like Girl Crazy Like

Boy crazy like the way you dress, so solid. Let me confess. I've been checking you out. Couldn't help myself. Look in my eyes. I blush. I get shy. Put on a saddle. I'm ready to horseback ride. How tall he is—five ten to six feet, some inches. Got me biting my lips, thinking. My frame against his ribs. Gave me two options: I can slide to mine or follow him to the crib. Rocka-hi, baby. I'm your new lady. I'm skipping one and choosing two. I always sleep alone. Tonight I'm going home with you. Boy crazy like I'm grown. Answer that in no time flat. Never mind that. Chemical balance, the sorcerer and the witch, magic exploding where he lives- Boy crazy like your voice. You're the top choice. Couldn't stop from making any noise. Damn near lost my poise. It's been a while since I've been this moist. Boy crazy like your ways. So insane. Thought it was my birthday.

Girl crazy like he's fiending for me. Ain't seen nothing this hot on TV. Body crazy like did somebody turn the heat up? Shocked his mind when I sucked down the last drop in the shot cup. I'm the dough girl, out the oven, golden and ready—spread the butter on with your machete. Girl crazy like he's thinking about the things I could do to him. Knows I get it in at the gym. Caught him the other day, standing there watching. In his twenties all over again. The fire started last night, blazed through the morning. He fell asleep—no snoring. I'm touching his coffee bean skin, feeling like something yummy in a bowl, all these good things caressing our souls. We're spooning, music in the background. Took many years before this was found. He better believe, like the stiches in his sleeves. She's inside out, double knotted down. Got up five hours later, showered, got dressed, and left. She did him the best. She's popping. She's on her way for her facial and some shopping. Girl crazy like the pics of her- Boy crazy like remembering his number- He keeps playing in her mind like a love movie, so smile. Next thing we know we're on each other's favorite list to dial.

She's boy crazy like. He's girl crazy like. We go berserk over them, excited infatuation, a little nervous, heartbeat racing, trying to keep it all under control, no chasing. Internal restraining order—let's just stand here and loiter. I got antsy and couldn't resist any longer. Can I get a dollar for these four quarters? I'm wondering if you can give back what I put in, something like … hmmm, yeah, that's right, 100 percent. You do me, and I do you. I'll be the most loyal in your crew. It's a long time overdue. We're the best to choose. Don't need to look anymore. We've met before. Knew right then I was gonna be yours. Make it easy or hard—it's your pick. We can stay or get on with it. She's boy crazy like wondering if this is too quick. He's girl crazy like she's the perfect fit.

Awww Man All Man

I gotta man who's awww man, all man.

His plan got that confidence can.

Never seen him in skinny jeans. I guess his four, five, or nine won't fit,

not enough room for the third leg to kick up to rest.

His style leans back for the headrest.

Okay, red curtains, red behind the headboard, red sheets, red candles lit,

red bone, bedroom playlist,

chill flow, no light coming from the window.

We're California dreaming,

sedated from the worst fiending.

All week going for hours, now we're all weak,

kissing my lips and my cheek—affectionate disrespect.

How wild do we get?

F U for feeling so good.

Make me squint my eyes and throw that phrase back in his face.

Hardwood

in my walls and my floors, he keeps moving forward.

He must want some more.

Squeeze the trigger on his gun even tighter.

I'm not religious, but out of nowhere I turned pious.

On the front line going up against Goliath,

I'm his number one fighter,

intermission and pass him the apple cider,

expert with the work—you know it hurts—

apologizing for pushing the pain,

the sting, the euphoria. Do you relate?

We're insane. No dope. It's dope I mean—

dopamine.

Together we're deadlier than overdosing on heroin and cocaine.

He came dying while saying my name.

That's sex fame.

Tried to get up, but I couldn't stand.

Awww man, all man.

Diamond Kiss Thoughts

I love what comes out of his mouth,
but
when I see him
I'ma suck the words
from his throat
till I choke on his verbs
and understand what he's thinking about.

Sweet Dirty Secrets

I told you all my sweet dirty secrets.
Now you're my sweet dirty secret.
Do you think you can keep it?
Addicts get sick when their drugs aren't injected.
Intervention and the desire to quit ar-
en't enough when the brain is reckless.
Crashes never stop halfway, only when it's time for the wrecker.
Call the insurance company.
I'm totaled.
They'll never be able to get me back.
I'm spoiled.
Indian hair grows from my roots on my back halfway around my neck.
Go ahead, grab, and pull.
I'm not worried about anything coming out or getting my hair wet.
I'll just take a shower with you after we sweat,
silky flesh when you caress,
the poshest you ever felt—you'll never forget
jewels in the chest.
How long do you think we're gonna run? Till I say I'm done.
I'm confidently insecure. My heart is filthy pure.
If I said I'll do it, I'm pretty sure.
I can't get enough of how you pick the pits out of my core.
I gotta have some more. I love the way you
split my peach behind closed doors,
beating my head against the shoe boxes on the closet floor.
We made it through war
so we could love some more.

Body Diamond

Body diamond got my eyes shining.
The way you fit on me got my body grinding.
You go so deep in my earth, seems like you're diamond mining.
Body diamond.
What you've been looking for, for sure you're finding.
Love and lust are blinding, everything perfect with the best timing.
You're tame, you don't break, you understand my mistakes.
You protect me from the fakes. When it comes
to being there, you don't hesitate.
Cool and chill by the way you appear.
Body diamond, you bring heat when you are near.
Can anyone imagine an energy encased in a form so brilliant?
Came from the universe to my world like we
were always meant—to be or not.
How did we get so hot, taking shots and gambling on these Vegas slots,
keeping our focus on winning the jackpot?
Because getting back a little is not enough
when the stakes are up with everything you got,
so give me diamonds all across my machine,
body cut and clean.
Say you love me and I'm what you need,
and I'll never pawn you to someone else.
I'll keep you close as my greatest wealth.
My body is my temple.
You are a part of my house.

I Really Love You

Her: Boy, I really love you.
That's why I wait patiently for you to come home to me.
Boy, I really love you. That's why I give you that peace and harmony.
Boy, I really love you. That's why my heart aches
and sometimes I cry myself to sleep.
Boy, I really love you. That's why nobody can get close to me.
I love my family, but there isn't anybody like my baby.
Boy, I really love you. I know you're out there, try-
ing to take care of everything.
Boy, I really love you, and that's why I'll be
right here when you look for me.
It's like you bring out all this love I have hidden in
me, so I share it with you in the purest way.

Him: Girl, I really love you.
I know you're loyal and won't leave my side.
Wish I was there to see you content—all smiles, never any cries.
Girl, I really love you, something I think in be-
tween my thoughts in those meetings,
on the plane—domestic, international, pri-
vate, commercial—conference calls,
all over the place.
I'd rather be at home, rubbing your back after breakfast in bed,
but I'm working hard instead,
keeping you living well and away from debt.
Girl, I really love you. You know you're the best.
That's why I'm coming home to you,
a break from all this chaos and stress.

I Need You to Fight for Me

I need you to fight for me. I'm not trying to be violent, but how are you going to know if I stay silent? I need you there if it gets popping, like if we're out all night rocking and a dude disrespects and starts his plotting. I'm not interested, so I keep walking. If he calls me ho or a trick, I hope you are the type to punch him with your fists- too smart to get caught and arrested- I'm with you and need to feel safe, protected from the wolves attempting to chew my flesh and drink the blood out of my face. Your guns may be too much and my Mace not enough. I'm feminine. I'm not that tough. My gentleman is rough. I mind my business. I'm not the drama type. When it gets down to it, I guard my cubs with my life, but for me, I need my lion king to fight.

I need you to fight for me. Would you let me go so easy? I thought I was your baby. Hold up. I am your girl, so why would you let me slip back into that grimy world, like it ain't nothing? You're irrationally accepting someone else is something, or you think that I would be all alone. Taking for granted or being nonchalant puts you in a danger zone. Sitting on the fence like Humpty Dumpty swinging his legs on the wall, Humpty Dumpty lost his yoke in the fall. I scrambled him up with some toast and ate him all. Now Humpty Dumpty is gone. I need you to fight for me like there is no other choice for us. Tell me I'm the only woman you ever loved, that the others … What others? They never existed. Living in a fantasy, along comes the realist. I need you to fight for me. Act crazy if I hint I might go. Stalk me and blow up my phone. Do anything, but don't leave me alone. Don't, don't, don't leave me alone.

Jungle Boy

Jungle boy, come get me.
I know you're around.
Quietly stalk me, as creepy as it sounds.
I stop breathing.
My heart is pumping too loud.
I do … I don't … I do … maybe wanna be found.
These poisonous spiders, beautiful snakes, dangerous frogs
I always seem to escape.
Jumping over mossy logs,
you must be a jaguar.
You're too wild to be a dog.
I feel your heat
fast through the green,
beneath the canopy.
Run,
jungle boy.
Come capture your hon.

Oil Spill

I'm suffering from severe insecurities
you wouldn't believe.
I'm getting my wants confused with my needs.
They're looking, but they can't see.
Smiling,
I only see teeth.
Well, it takes the end of the mouth to touch the cheeks
to impress me.
Now these wolves give me the creeps,
stepping forward to snatch out my throat
so that I can't speak,
then rip out my heart
to stop the beat!
Please!
My pretty red lipstick
looks like bloed smeared in his beard after we kiss,
gold glitter here and there on his outfit,
dirty, stinking, filthy, ugly,
rich,
and his hands are all over my face, ass, and tits.
Oh,
he couldn't resist
bending me over and squeezing my hips,
pulling my hair in his fists,
losing control.
Where did the moments go?
He went to law school in London.
He hails from Lagos.
It's a wild private show
All of curtains are closed on the windows.

Now we're ready.
He's swinging my legs around like machetes,
Underclothes, striped socks, studded shoes thrown across the room—
I'm the oil getting drilled by this tycoon.

Love Grains of Sand

It's me …
These sheets,
my pillows under my titties, the remote control near my feet,
and a duvet covering half my body.
One o'clock to 5:30 a.m.—I should be asleep,
but I'm awake, going back and forth in my brain,
mapping out the details of what needs to get done.
Then I'm wondering what I should do with you, hon.
Settle on quitting and try to run.
You sent a message back of "lol," like I'm fun.
Could I be the joke or am I too serious?
We used to be curious.
We went all in till we were knocked out and delirious.
We are selfish.
Made a few people furious.
I keep snapping back in your hands like a rubber band.
Awww, man, I'm in trouble land.
All I can give you is some love, patience, space, and try to understand
With no real future ties,
we live our own lives,
get together whenever we can,
like waves crashing onto the beach in the sand.
You're gone.
Traces that you were here have fossilized in me and dried
till the next you come back and flood my life.
This happens every time you roll in with the tide.

Tan Bands

Look at my wrists—rubber tan bands for the
cash that I can't stuff in my fists.
When I die,
cremate me naked with yellow, black, and red garter belts on my thighs,
at least one over the Indian head.
Place it exactly the way I did when I was alive.
Sprinkle rose petals on both of my breasts,
a couple bars of gold to melt on the bones and the flesh,
golden-gray ash to put in a diamond locket for my men.
Think of me when I was breathing.
I was thinking of them every evening,
kept them like jewels in a safe and well protected.
My instinct is to act in any given second,
no questions asked, no questions answered.
They take note of the quick flash, of my expression.
I acknowledge. I pay attention
to everything going on. Very little is a surprise.
I keep it vibrant and fly as high as the sky.
You can see me standing next to the stars side by side.
I came by myself, and I didn't drive.
I'll probably be smoking and drinking till they turn on the lights.
Now that I'm blind as a bat, he wants to give me a ride.
Okay,
he's taking me home.
He's been there many times—fifteen steps stumble to my
place by seventeen minutes-I'm unlocking the door.
I'm still not alone, going so fast.
How did I lose my clothes?
Kissing me this way, I think he's trying to get me to fall in love.
Sticking me like this, he's getting rough. He couldn't get out.
Kept him for a year or so, then I finally loosened my grip,
sent him back to the girl he used to be with.

Wanted Magic

You want some of my magic?
I've got that wicked voodoo for you.
I bring all kinds of wild situations and moods through.
Be careful how you bite—it might be more than you can chew.
Erzulie Freda bracelet on my wrist,
got Lakshmi on my chest.
Honor the trees and my relatives who rest.
I give and request the best:
rose champagne, caviar, beef carpaccio, and tuna tartar.
Better believe I'm used to this.
Give your ex her last kiss. All these candles lit,
I hex that chick.
I'm a bit narcissistic and can be a selfish witch,
but I'll king you just so you praise me.
That's the way it goes with a God and her followers.
Call me crazy. I'm a deity. I've been picked by them.
Crossing from the heavens,
Six, two –eight, seven- seven,
thanks to my ancestors, I am their descendant.
You want some of my magic.
I've got that wicked voodoo for you.
Give me what I like, and I can make all your wishes come true.
Unbelievable I know how to bring about the unexplained
happiness that can take your breath away.
It's not good if it ain't great.
It's not raining if it doesn't flood the lakes.
It's not tight if it don't gives the chills and the shakes.
Nothing's free when time is money; we all gotta pay.
Dancing amongst the stars till the sun breaks,
I got that homemade icing for the cake.

Sculptures

Take it off, take it off. Get naked, raw, and sweaty.
You got my mind tricked out like johns in
Chevys looking for … Ugly Betty.
Are you ready?
One drink, two drinks, three drinks, and a little more,
all our clothes got lost all over the house floors.
Maybe I forgot to lock the door,
stumbled to the alarm, and pressed a few numbers and then a four.
So much going on—how did I end up on the sink
with all this pounding? I can't … I can't … I can't fucking think.
Blink.
I'm breathing hard.
You got more horsepower than supercharge.
You know who you are.
The smile promised you were gonna give it to me before we left the bar.
Dropped all guards,
one minute out of the parking lot in the car.
Went so crazy, almost gave that thang a passion mark.
What we do we do it in the dark.
What you do?
You do break my ice heart.
Bang and shattered—
How could you go and destroy me like it don't matter?

A Story for Our Souls

Get all the way out and let the world spin. Take a trip around the oceans close to the heavens, in between the dead and the living. Outside the body let's look at ourselves together. The way we hold hands and smile might motivate others or could make them jealous. We don't care about the ladies or the fellas who try to separate us for themselves. We're blind as bats. We only feel our heat. In large crowds we can hear the others whisper when we speak. You lean into me to say something sweet. I move my waist next to yours. You smell so good to me. We can see my lips moving, telling you this. It looks like we wanna kiss. We don't do it, at least not yet.

You're asking me how my day went. You never stop watching me with genuine interest. I tell you that it was crazy. I need a drink. You laugh at how dramatic I act and nod your head to the bartender. Put what she wants on my tab. She brings back what I ask. Then we raise our drinks up to tap. I start saying some of the things on my mind. You're into me the whole time. What was bothering me disappears. Now I feel fine, as a stone coming fresh from the mine, cracking and brushing away the dirt. You know how to make me shine. We both watch as I tease you and say things to see how you respond. You get serious as your eyes and face change. I quickly say I would never do anything wrong. I love treating you right.

As we spectate from afar, we decide to get closer to who we are. It's about to happen, and we won't miss one detail of this part. Your eyes follow behind every step I make as I walk. I speed up. I slow the pace to spin around. You've run into me at the last minute. I get the keys to open the door. A drink, a shower, a few more words—it's about to occur, and I'm doing everything I can to calm you down, but I never heard of someone stopping a tsunami or the thundering beyond the clouds. I was dry and now the sheets, you, and I are wet. Shoes, clothes, belts, and earrings are thrown wherever they land.

My oasis has been turned into a wonderful mess, wild and intense. It's a while before we stop. Waves of warmth keep hitting me, but give you the chills. We've fallen back into our bodies. We both rock into each other. It's back and forth, kissing as if we're trying to have our last meals. You finally break. You are no longer crashing against me, but are resting as relaxed as the sea along the beach. What did we come to earth for? To experience this in the flesh. The Gods and the immortals would be envious of this.

Lady

Hey, baby, I'll be your lady,
the kind of lady that holds herself well,
knows when to give you space or if you need to be held.
I used to be a bad B, outspoken, and all out.
I changed my ways and keep a lot more to myself.
I'd rather be your lady, soft-spoken with excellent etiquette,
wear suits designed by St. John and Chanel, dress
more like Oprah and the wife of the president.
First Lady of the House—
no more time for crazy parties or wild nights on the town.
I'm getting tickets to watch symphonic operas on my way to polo matches,
NASCAR racing, getting a big hat to wear to the Kentucky Derby.
I have to see a rodeo show at least one time.
As you can tell, I have a few things on my mind.
No more extensions, it's all mine.
Short manicured nails in nude, red, or light pink—
I hope you like it. I care what you think.
Hey, baby, I'll be your lady,
the kind of female that makes you smile really proud.
No more cursing—they don't come out of my mouth.
All loyalty without any doubts,
Bad chicks bare nudes for social media likes.
I only want your attention and nobody else.
Hey, baby, I'll be your lady.

Thank You

Thank you
for
the
truth.
Do you think I'm crazy?
Most geniuses are.
I do not know which, or both, I might be.
You must have known
I belong to the world.
Even if it hurts,
life
is
perfect.

End Matter

Gordona Bloe (pronounced Gor•don•a Bloo) introduces *Tough Cotton*, which is a series of thoughts and experiences that are expressed in poetry, lyrics, and short stories. *Tough Cotton* is chaotic, dramatic, tumultuous, intense, and edgy. Love, lust, and passion vibrate throughout the scenes of *Tough Cotton*. Life begins on and in the earth. "Cotton Seeds" is a voice to the youth and perhaps ourselves, found or lost. "Bloeming" (pronounced Blooming) is recognition of who Tough Cotton is becoming or rejecting to become. "Ginned" goes into the underworld of drugs and prison. It is where all is separated. Storms and thorns flood and shake *Tough Cotton*. "Wrinkled Sheets" embodies the passion, heat, and comfort. She refuses to succumb to the disasters that would prevent her from reaching her ultimate goal of what she is meant to be or rather what she always was. ... and that is Tough Cotton.

Made in the USA
Middletown, DE
16 July 2021

44294313R00083